WRITE YOUR OWN

FAIRY TALE

by Natalie M. Rosinsky

Compass Point Books ✦ Minneapolis, Minnesota

Compass Point Books
3109 West 50th Street, #115
Minneapolis, MN 55410

This book was manufactured with paper containing
at least 10 percent post-consumer waste.

Managing Editor: Catherine Neitge
Designer: ticktock Entertainment Ltd
Page Production: Bobbie Nuytten
Photo Researcher: Svetlana Zhurkin
Library Consultant: Kathleen Baxter

Art Director: Jaime Martens
Creative Director: Keith Griffin
Editorial Director: Nick Healy

Compass Point Books would like to acknowledge the contributions of Tish Farrell, who
authored earlier Write Your Own books and whose supporting text is reused in part herein.

Library of Congress Cataloging-in-Publication Data
Rosinsky, Natalie M. (Natalie Myra)
  Write your own fairy tale / by Natalie M. Rosinsky.
    p. cm. — (Write your own)
  Includes index.
  ISBN-13: 978-0-7565-3369-4 (library binding)
  ISBN-10: 0-7565-3369-4 (library binding)
  1. Fairy tales—Authorship. I. Title. II. Series.
PN3377.5.F32R67 2008
808'.066398—dc22   2007015720

Visit Compass Point Books on the Internet at *www.compasspointbooks.com*
or e-mail your request to *custserv@compasspointbooks.com*

About the Author
Natalie M. Rosinsky is the award-winning author of
more than 100 works for young readers. She earned
graduate degrees from the University of Wisconsin-
Madison and has been a high school teacher and
college professor as well as a corporate trainer. Natalie,
who reads and writes in Mankato, Minnesota, says,
"My love of reading led me to write. I take pleasure in
framing ideas, crafting words, detailing other lives and
places. I am delighted to share these joys with young
authors in the Write Your Own series of books."

Your Spellbinding Adventure

Are you ready for a spellbinding adventure? Fairy tales transport readers to magical places where good battles evil and heroic deeds are done. Fantastic creatures inhabit these fairy-tale worlds, where supernatural events happen during everyday life. Often someone in the tale lives happily ever—though what finally makes that character happy is sometimes surprising!

You, too, can enchant readers with fairy tales that you write. This book contains brainstorming and training activities that will work like a charm to sharpen your writing skills. Tips and advice from famous writers and examples from their own work will help you to cast a spell over readers. Your imagination will be your magic wand!

CONTENTS

WANT TO BE A WRITER?

This book is the perfect place to start. It aims to give you the tools to write your own fairy tales. Learn how to craft believable portraits of people and perfect plots with satisfying beginnings, middles, and endings. Examples from famous books appear throughout, with tips and techniques from published authors to help you on your way.

Get the writing habit

Do timed and regular practice. Real writers learn to write even when they don't particularly feel like it.

Create a fairy tale-writing zone.

Keep a journal.

Carry a notebook—record interesting events and note how people behave and speak.

Generate ideas

Find a fairy tale you want to tell or retell. Who are its characters, and what are their problems?

Brainstorm to find out everything about your chosen fairy tale.

Research settings, events, and people related to the fairy tale.

Plan

What is your fairy tale about?

What happens?

Plan beginning, middle, and end.

Write a synopsis or create storyboards.

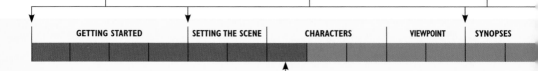

GETTING STARTED | SETTING THE SCENE | CHARACTERS | VIEWPOINT | SYNOPSES

You can follow your progress by using the bar located on the bottom of each page. The orange color tells you how far along the fairy tale writing process you have gotten. As the blocks are filled out, your fairy tale will be growing.

Write

Write the first draft, then put it aside for a while.

Check spelling and dialogue—does it flow?

Remove unnecessary words.

Does the fairy tale have a good title and satisfying ending?

Avoid clichés that do not suit your purpose.

Publish

Write or print the final draft.

Always keep a copy for yourself.

Send your fairy tale to children's magazines, Internet writing sites, competitions, or school magazines.

| AND PLOTS | WINNING WORDS | SCINTILLATING SPEECH | HINTS AND TIPS | THE NEXT STEP |

When you get to the end of the bar, your book is ready to go! You are an author! You now need to decide what to do with your book and what your next project should be. Perhaps it will be a sequel to this fairy tale, or maybe something completely different.

YOUR ENCHANTING LIFESTYLE

What tales have already been told about brave princes, beautiful princesses, and magic spells? Are there more stories about hidden treasures, enchanted creatures, and wicked witches? Find out by doing research in the library or on the Internet. When you sit down to write your tales, just like any writer you will need handy tools and a safe, comfortable place for your work. A computer can make writing quicker, but it is not essential. Your imagination can work wonders even with simpler tools.

What you need

These materials will help you organize your ideas and your findings:

- small notebook that you carry everywhere
- paper for writing activities
- pencils or pens with different colored ink
- index cards for recording facts
- files or folders to keep your gathered information organized and safe
- dictionary, thesaurus, and encyclopedia

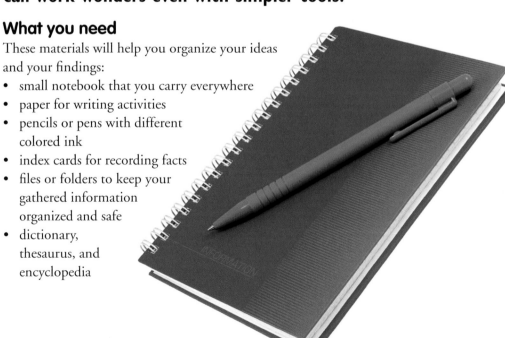

Find your writing place

Think about where you as a writer feel most comfortable and creative. Perhaps a spot in your bedroom works best for you. Possibly a corner in the public library is better. If your writing place is outside your home, store your writing materials in a take-along bag or backpack.

Create a fairy tale-writing zone

- Play some of your favorite music or music associated with fairy tales.
- Use earplugs if you write best when it is quiet.
- Decorate your space with pictures of fairy tale characters or of places associated with fairy tales.
- Place objects that hold good memories from your own life around your space.

Follow the writer's golden rule

Once you have chosen your writing space, go there regularly and often. It is all right to do other kinds of writing there—such as a diary or letters—as long as you *keep on writing*!

CASE STUDY

Philip Pullman (right) writes by hand in his study at home. He works every morning and afternoon, with breaks for coffee and stretching and getting out. His day's work is done when he has completed 1,000 words or three handwritten pages.

Robin McKinley uses a laptop computer to write between two and 14 hours daily. As her book takes shape, the amount of time she writes each day increases.

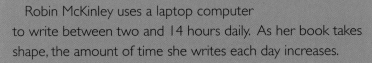

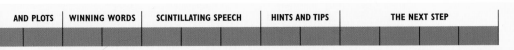

Before you can write fabulous fairy tales, you have to build up your writing "muscles." Just as an athlete lifts weights or a musician practices scales, you must train regularly. You cannot wait until you are in the mood or feel inspired.

Tips and techniques

Set a regular amount of time and a schedule for your writing. It could be 10 minutes every morning before breakfast or one hour twice a week after supper. Then, come rain or shine, stick to your schedule.

Now it's your turn

Tell it with a twist!

Some modern fairy tale writers add a twist to old tales. They change the traditional hero or villain in some way, or provide an unexpected setting or ending. Some of these "fractured" fairy tales contain several twists and are often funny. Tickle your funny bone—but not enough to break it—by reading a fractured fairy tale or two.

Now brainstorm ways in which you might twist a fairy tale. Spend 10 minutes jotting down strange or silly substitutions, surprising settings, and entertaining endings. If this exercise leaves your eyes gleaming like a dragon's golden treasure, you may have fun writing your own fractured fairy tale.

Now it's your turn

To be fair

Explore another side of a traditional fairy tale. We all know about Cinderella's suffering at the hands of her cruel step-mother and stepsisters. But how did the rat feel after being magically transformed into a coachman? Philip Pullman writes this story in *I Was a Rat!*

Brainstorm about the characters in a fairy tale you enjoy. What would a background character have to say about its events? What would this character find important or interesting? Take 10 minutes to jot down ideas. These might be the inspiration for your new version of a familiar tale.

Tips and techniques

Virginia Hamilton urged writers to "carry a notebook with you at all times. That way you'll never miss an important moment."

CASE STUDY

Vivian Vande Velde wrote a collection of stories titled *Tales from the Brothers Grimm and the Sisters Weird.* She says, "I really enjoyed playing with all those fairy tales, turning things on their heads, making the character usually thought of as the villain be the good guy, or starting earlier than the traditional story starts, or going on beyond the usual end."

FIND YOUR VOICE

Being a good reader is the magic ingredient to becoming a good writer. Reading will help you develop your writer's voice—a style of writing that is all your own. It takes much practice to acquire this unique voice. Writers continue to develop their voices throughout their lives. Skilled writers also learn to change their voices to match different subjects.

Finding your writer's voice

When you read as a writer, you notice the range and rhythm of different authors' words and sentences. Vivian Vande Velde uses more casual words than Charles Perrault does. Alan Garner captures the rhythm of people talking in the English countryside. Learning to recognize how different writers craft their stories is like learning to identify different types of music.

Experiment

You may usually read only fantasies or fairy tales. Try other genres to see how authors of mysteries or adventure stories, for instance, write with their own unique voices. You might get writing tips by reading about the adventures of Arthur Conan Doyle's famous detective Sherlock Holmes.

Writers' voices

Look at the words and sentences these writers use. Which writer uses short as well as long sentences? Do you think this choice works well? Which writer has a character talking? Was this an effective choice? Which writers use old-fashioned language?

> *Beast was looking at the man skeptically. "Your daughter's name is Beauty?" he asked. "What kind of name is that? What did you do, call her 'Hey, you,' until she grew up, and then, when she turned out to be good-looking, you finally settled on a name for her? Or did you call her Beauty from the start, simply hoping for the best, trusting to chance that she wouldn't turn out to be a dog?"*
> Vivian Vande Velde, "Beast and Beauty," in *Tales from the Brothers Grimm and the Sisters Weird*

> *There were once a king and a queen who were very upset that they had no children at all, more upset than words can say. They went all over the world, taking the waters, making vows and pilgrimages, and performing every devotion. They tried everything and nothing seemed to work. At last, however, the queen became pregnant and gave birth to a daughter. The king and queen had scoured the land for seven fairies to stand as godmothers for the little princess, and each gave her a gift as was the custom with fairies in those days. In this way, the princess could acquire every perfection.*
> Charles Perrault, "The Sleeping Beauty," in *The Complete Fairy Tales of Charles Perrault*

> *Words rose in me, filled my mouth, pushed against my lips. Yes, I'll marry you. Yes, I love you. Yes! Yes! Yes!*
> Gail Carson Levine, *Ella Enchanted*

> *Next day, that there little thing looked so maliceful when it came for the flax. And at night, she heard it knocking against the window panes. She opened the window, and it came right in on the ledge. It was grinning from ear to ear, and oh! its tail was twirling around so fast.*
> Alan Garner, "Tom Tit Tot," in *Alan Garner's Book of British Fairy Tales*

GET YOUR FACTS STRAIGHT

Often traditional fairy tales are set in the distant past. If you are writing about people who lived long ago, use the library or Internet to get your facts straight. For example, what kinds of buttons, ribbons, and boots would a princess have worn? What kind of clothing would a peasant have worn? If you are using a particular location, which livestock—sheep, goats, or cattle—do farmers raise there? What kinds of fish swim in its rivers? A farmer and an expert angler might be good resource people to ask.

Now it's your turn

Just like a fairy tale!

Increase your knowledge of traditional fairy tales. Look at collections of tales by the Brothers Grimm, Charles Perrault, or Hans Christian Andersen. Or pick up *One Thousand and One Arabian Nights* for fairy tales from another continent. Find and read at least three tales that you have not heard of before.

In your writing place, use pen and paper to brainstorm about these and other fairy tales. What do they have in common? What do you like most or least about them? You may have just found the fairy tale elements for your own story!

Now it's your turn

Explore the world of fairy tales

Some fairy tale favorites such as Cinderella are told all around the globe. Find and read a version of this story from another culture or part of the world. What does this version add to the tale you know? Does your family or community have traditions that you could add to your own fairy tale favorite?

Take 10 minutes to brainstorm. Jot down details about special holiday traditions or the ways new babies, birthdays, or weddings are celebrated. Do not worry about grammar or spelling—just let the ideas flow freely like delicious juice from a magic pitcher. You are on your way to being a writer of fairy tales!

CASE STUDY

In *The Prince of the Pond*, Donna Jo Napoli writes about a prince transformed by a witch into a frog. To get her facts straight, Napoli researched the biology of frogs in the library. She also visited a nearby pond and spent hours watching frogs, insects, and other creatures there.

CASE STUDY

Robert D. San Souci has written several Cinderella stories set in different cultures. He found echoes of such traditional tales all around the world. San Souci says that in his stories, "I try to share that sense of discovery and delight in how much alike and yet how wonderfully different are so many peoples."

Tips and techniques

Transform your own "pumpkins" into "magic coaches." If you recently felt angry, nervous, or disappointed about something, use those experiences to help you choose or add life to your fairy tale.

A WORLD OF WONDERS

In your fairy tales, you reveal a world full of wonders. Your setting may be traditional or modern. Its everyday scenes will seem sharper, brighter, and clearer through the many details you describe. Readers will feel as though they are right there—even without having had fairy dust sprinkled on their eyes! Your wonderful attention to detail and imagination will also help you create scenes of magical places and events that are impossible in the real world.

Sensational nature

Use as many of the five senses as you can to bring a scene to life. Penny Pollock does this in her retelling of one Native American version of Cinderella. Readers can smell, hear, see, and feel this tale set in the American Southwest.

> *The Turkey Girl caught the excitement, imagining herself dancing with the others. Rich odors of the feast would rise from the fires. A pulsing beat would fill the air. Dancers in bright colors would circle together. … Water from her jug sloshed onto her tattered shawl, ending her daydream. She had no place at the dance. She was just the Turkey Girl, clad in rags.*
> Penny Pollock, *The Turkey Girl: A Zuni Cinderella Story*

In her retelling of "Beauty and the Beast," Donna Jo Napoli adds taste to her "sensational" description of a lush palace garden in Persia. Readers can taste as well as see the fruit on the cherry trees.

> *The air is faint with white jasmine. Clover and aromatic grasses crush soft under my bare feet. Sour cherry trees fan out in star designs.*
> Donna Jo Napoli, *Beast*

Now it's your turn

Be sensational!

Many traditional fairy tales have scenes set outdoors—in forests or near mountains, caves, ponds, or the ocean. Visit the nearest green spot with your writer's notebook in hand. Look around. Close your eyes and breathe deeply. Listen carefully. Run your hand through the grass or along a tree trunk. Now take 10 minutes to jot down all the details your senses revealed. Use these details as you create a fairy tale world for readers.

Be surprising!

You may choose to set your fairy tale in an unusual place. New York City in the 1900s is the setting for Arthur Levine's *The Boardwalk Princess*. This tale follows the adventures of an orphaned brother and sister. Jackie Mims Hopkins' *The Horned Toad Prince* is set "on the lonesome prairie" of Texas. Even though these settings are unexpected, the authors use vivid details to bring scenes to life.

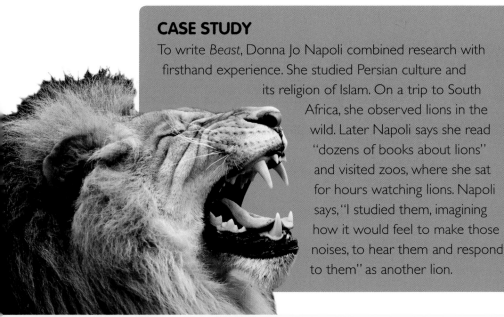

CASE STUDY

To write *Beast*, Donna Jo Napoli combined research with firsthand experience. She studied Persian culture and its religion of Islam. On a trip to South Africa, she observed lions in the wild. Later Napoli says she read "dozens of books about lions" and visited zoos, where she sat for hours watching lions. Napoli says, "I studied them, imagining how it would feel to make those noises, to hear them and respond to them" as another lion.

CREATING IMPOSSIBLE SETTINGS

Fairy tales often include settings and actions that are impossible in the real world. Gail Carson Levine's fractured version of the Cinderella story contains both.

In *Cinderellis and the Glass Hill*, the hero must climb a glass hill as big as an ancient Egyptian pyramid! Levine's real-life comparisons make this impossible situation real for her readers:

> In a week the pyramid was built. Its glass was clearer than a drop of dew and slipperier than the sides of an ice cube. … Cinderellis saw the glass hill from a mile and a half away, sparkling in the sunlight. It was as high and almost as steep as the castle's highest tower.
> Gail Carson Levine, *Cinderellis and the Glass Hill*

When Cinderellis first touches the hill, it feels "lovely—cool and smoother than smooth." When his hand keeps sliding off it, though, all the startled young man can think is "Whoops!" Having Cinderellis use this ordinary expression is another way the author makes this extraordinary situation real for readers.

Tips and techniques
Use everyday language and comparisons to make magical situations and places seem real to readers.

In her version of "Hansel and Gretel," Donna Jo Napoli uses tasty details to show how the witch's candy cottage attracts the two children:

> *Bright red buttery caramels form a cornice on every window. Palest of jellied gumdrops stick up in cone-shaped mounds along the roof. ... The entire log house is decorated with candies.* Donna Jo Napoli, *The Magic Circle*

Even though rain or snow would destroy such a cottage, Napoli's mouthwatering details make this impossible setting seem real to readers.

Now it's your turn

Do sensational research

Research in the library or on the Internet can also help you get a better sense of a faraway location or a nearby place in a different season. Look for:

- photographs taken in different seasons
- lists of wildlife that live there in different seasons
- recordings of wildlife sounds
- written descriptions of locations, wildlife, and changing seasons

Take notes on details that you can use in your own fairy tales.

DISCOVER YOUR HERO

Traditional fairy tales spotlight brave, generous, and kind young people. Their virtues help them conquer evil and win their hearts' desires. Your hero may be one of these figures—or you may decide to focus on a minor character or even someone who is usually the villain. Whatever your choice, your job is to make readers care about this person and his or her problems.

Tell your hero's problems

Perhaps your hero—like the Frog Prince or Beast—has been magically transformed into a creature. Perhaps—like Sleeping Beauty—she needs to be rescued from the effects of an evil spell. In Gail Carson Levine's fairy tale novel, Ella suffers from a spell that makes her obey every command:

> If someone told me to hop on one foot for a day and a half, I'd have to do it. And hopping on one foot wasn't the worst order I could be given. If you commanded me to cut off my own head, I'd have to do it.
> I was in danger at every moment.
> Gail Carson Levine, *Ella Enchanted*

In this novel, though, Ella finds a way to rescue herself! Just like Beauty in "Beauty and the Beast," her strong character saves the day.

Perhaps your hero faces a seemingly impossible task—such as turning straw into gold in "Rumpelstiltskin" or "Tom Tit Tot." Often fairy tale heroes go on dangerous journeys and overcome three perils.

Find a good name

The right name for your hero will work its own magic. By naming her male hero Ellis, Gail Carson Levine lets readers know right away that *Cinderellis and the Glass Hill* is a fractured version of Cinderella. This time, though, it is a princess who comes looking for the dirty-faced, overworked hero. Jay Williams gives readers a similar clue in *Petronella*. There, Princess Petronella—instead of Prince Peter—boldly goes off to have adventures and rescues a prince in distress.

In *The Magic Circle*, Donna Jo Napoli deliberately never names her central character—the woman who turns out to be the witch in "Hansel and Gretel." Everyone just calls this hunchbacked woman the Ugly One. This cruel nickname helps readers better understand the woman's love of beautiful things—a weakness that leads to her terrible fate.

Give your hero weaknesses

No one is perfect. One way to encourage readers to care about your hero is to show this character's flaws. Cinderellis wants his brothers' approval so much that he never complains or fights back. Napoli's prince in *Beast* is changed into a beast because he is too proud.

Tips and techniques
Have other characters tell what your hero looks like. Or have the hero describe his or her own reflection in a mirror, pool, or window.

Now it's your turn

"Magic" your hero into being

Use your imagination to brainstorm your hero into being. Draw five lines down a sheet of paper. Write one of these words at the top of each column: appearance, likes, dislikes, weaknesses, strengths, past experiences. Now take 10 to 15 minutes to think up five items for each category.

You now know 30 things about your hero! You may use all or only some of this information in your tale. Perhaps these ideas will lead you to others.

CREATE YOUR VILLAIN

Your villain creates the problem or conflict facing the hero. Yet not all villains are evil. Sometimes—as you may know from real life—problems are caused by people with good intentions. This is important to remember as you create a villain who challenges your hero.

What is the motive?

In fairy tales, people and supernatural creatures commit evil deeds for different reasons. They may be motivated by greed, jealousy, revenge, or even loneliness. They may believe that their deeds are not evil at all. In *Ella Enchanted*, the fairy Lucinda thinks she has given Ella the "gift" of obedience. Create a believable villain by showing this character's motives.

Some fairy tale villains

A wicked witch:

She takes revenge on a prince who trespassed by changing him into a frog:

> *"Ha. I showed you, didn't I? No matter where you are now, you're not safe. Anyone and anything can hurt you. And no one will ever think you are handsome or jaunty again. Ha ha ha ha."*
> Donna Jo Napoli, *The Prince of the Pond*

A greedy and self-centered father:

Ella's father does not think of her feelings when he needs money:

> *"I shall have to sell you in a manner of speaking. You must marry so that we can be rich again."*
> Gail Carson Levine, *Ella Enchanted*

Tips and techniques

Complicated villains are fascinating! Give your villain several motives to make the tale and your hero's struggle more intense.

A powerful supernatural creature:

Tom Tit Tot demands a terrible price for spinning straw into gold for a young woman:

> *It looked out of the corners of its eyes, and it said, "I'll give you three guesses every night to guess my name; and if you haven't guessed it before the month's up, you shall be mine."*
> Alan Garner, "Tom Tit Tot," in *Alan Garner's Book of British Fairy Tales*

Cruel relatives and neighbors:

Everyone misunderstands and is cruel to someone they consider ugly:

> *Everyone picked on the ugly duckling. The ducks bit him, the hens pecked him, the girl who came to feed the poultry kicked him out of the way. Even his own brothers and sisters looked down on him, and jeered "Yah! Boo! Hope the cat gets you!"*
> Hans Christian Andersen,
> *The Ugly Duckling*

Now it's your turn

The picture of evil

What does your villain look like? Get ideas by looking through old photographs, magazines, and books. When you find a face that interests you, take five or 10 minutes to write a description of it. Repeat this process. Now reread your descriptions. Is your villain's appearance captured in one description? Perhaps you need to combine descriptions to create your villainous portrait.

DEVELOP A SUPPORTING CAST

You can tell readers much about your hero and villain by showing how they act with other characters. Perhaps the villain first reveals his or her true nature this way. Work your story-telling magic by developing a supporting cast of characters.

CASE STUDY

Robin McKinley says "Beauty and the Beast" is her favorite fairy tale because, when she was growing up in the 1950s, it was the only one "that didn't have the heroine waiting limply to be rescued by the hero." McKinley has written two novels based on this tale: *Beauty* (1978) and *Rose Daughter* (1997).

Fairy tale creatures

Vivid descriptions show not only how strange some creatures are, but also whether they are friendly:

> *The elves were the same height as humans. With their mossy hair and green skin tinged with orange for the coming autumn, they were no more frightening than a pumpkin vine.*
> Gail Carson Levine, *Ella Enchanted*

Sometimes dialogue introduces readers to the strange, frightening ways of less-friendly fairy tale figures:

> *The morning after I left the elves, an ogre woke me by poking me with a stick. "Wake up, Breakfast. How do you liked to be cooked? Bloody? Medium? Or done to a crisp?"*
> *Eight ogres surrounded me.*
> *"It will only hurt for a minute." My ogre (the one who woke me) stroked my cheek. "I'm a fast eater."*
> Gail Carson Levine, *Ella Enchanted*

Tips and techniques
Include humans, animals, and fairy tale creatures in your cast of characters. Make some characters memorable through what they say as well as how they look or act.

Human and animal characters

A few repeated phrases can also quickly introduce and explain human characters and their relationships. Cinderellis' brothers always agree with each other and disagree with him. One brother's opinion always immediately follows the other's in this fractured fairy tale:

> *They wouldn't even try his warm-slipper powder, which Cinderellis had invented just for them—to keep their feet warm on cold winter nights.*
> *"Don't want it," Ralph said.*
> *"Don't like it," Burt said.*
> Gail Carson Levine, *Cinderellis and the Glass Hill*

Your main characters' relationships with animals can also be important in your tale. Robin McKinley shows readers this in *Beauty*. Its title character has a strong bond with her loyal horse, Greatheart. At first, brave Greatheart is terrified by Beast. As Beauty learns to trust Beast, Greatheart comes to accept him, too.

CHOOSE A POINT OF VIEW

Before you write the first fantastic line of your tale, you must decide who is telling the story. Do you want readers to know all about the characters—what everyone is thinking, feeling, and doing? Or do you want to follow the thoughts and experiences of just one character—such as your hero? Perhaps you have decided to retell a tale from the viewpoint of the villain or a minor character. These decisions determine your fairy tale's point of view.

Omniscient viewpoint

Traditional fairy tales are usually told from the all-seeing and all-knowing—the omniscient—point of view. The storyteller or narrator describes what all the characters think and feel and also shares knowledge of events beyond the characters' knowledge. Such tales often begin with the words "Once upon a time" or "There was once."

Hans Christian Andersen began "Thumbelina" this way:

> *There was once a woman who wished very much to have a little child ...*

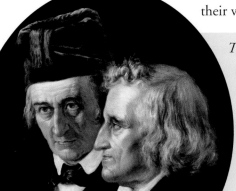

This is how the Brothers Grimm (left) begin their version of "Rumpelstiltskin":

There was once a Miller who was very poor, but he had a beautiful daughter. Now, it fell out that he had occasion to speak with the King, and, in order to give himself an air of importance, he said: "I have a daughter who can spin gold out of straw."
The Brothers Grimm, "Rumpelstiltskin," in *Grimm's Fairy Tales: Twenty Stories*

Diane Stanley retells the Rumpelstiltskin story with a twist, but she still uses the omniscient point of view:

Once there was a miller's daughter who got into a heap of trouble. It was all because her father liked to make up stories and pass them off as truth. Unfortunately, the story he told was that his daughter could spin straw into gold, which, of course, she could not. Even more unfortunately, he told this whopper in the hearing of a palace servant who rushed right off to tell the king.
Diane Stanley, *Rumpelstiltskin's Daughter*

FIRST-PERSON VIEWPOINT

The first-person viewpoint uses a character in the tale to narrate the story. This narrator uses words such as "I said" or "I thought" or "I did." Robin McKinley uses first-person viewpoint to have her hero, Beauty, narrate her own adventures. Similarly, Gail Carson Levine has Ella tell her own first-person story in *Ella Enchanted*.

There are other exciting possibilities for using the first-person viewpoint in fairy tales. Perhaps you will choose a minor character to narrate events. Donna Jo Napoli has a female frog in the pond tell the tale of a magically transformed prince:

> *He blinked. His skin looked strange. Almost dusty, like a toad's. But he was no toad.*
> *"What's the matter with your mucus glands?" I said.*
> *He twisted his upper body and thrust it forward, cocking his head.*
> *I had never seen a frog do that before. "Are you all right?"*
> Donna Jo Napoli, *The Prince of the Pond*

Now it's your turn

Magically switch viewpoints!
Think of a scene in your tale where the hero first meets or finally fights the villain. Write this scene from the hero's point of view. Now use the magic wand of your imagination to write this scene from the villain's viewpoint. Magically switch viewpoints again to rewrite this scene from the sidelines, using the viewpoint of a nearby person or animal. Reread your scenes. Which version do you like best? Allow half an hour for this activity.

Perhaps—as Napoli does in *The Magic Circle*—you will have a fairy tale villain such as the witch narrate events from a first-person viewpoint.

Third-person viewpoint

With the third-person viewpoint, the writer stays inside one character's mind but uses "he said" or "she thought" to describe events. This narrator can only tell what other characters think or feel through dialogue. Sometimes the narrator misunderstands events! Third-person viewpoint is often written in the past tense:

Reba Jo knew she should turn back. But right at the edge of this gully she spied a vulture, all fat and sassy, sitting on top of a dried-up old well, just daring her to toss her spinning rope around its long ugly neck.
Jackie Mims Hopkins, *The Horned Toad Prince*

TELL YOUR STORY'S STORY

As your fairy tale takes shape like a castle built by magical hands, it is a good idea to describe it in a paragraph or two. This is called a synopsis. If someone asked, "What is this tale about?" these paragraphs would be the answer. An editor often wants to see a synopsis of a story before accepting it for publication.

Study back cover blurbs

Studying the information on the back cover of a book—called the blurb—will help you write an effective synopsis. A good blurb contains a brief summary of a book's content. It also gives the tone of the book—whether it is serious or funny. Most important of all, the blurb makes readers want to open the book and read it cover to cover! That is certainly true of this blurb:

Now it's your turn

Announce it with flair!
Write a blurb for the fairy tale you plan to write. Summarizing it in one or two paragraphs will sharpen your ideas.

Every day, Reba Jo prowls the dusty prairie, roping critters and twanging her guitar. When the spunky cowgirl finds herself in a mess of trouble, only a pesky horned toad can save her hide. But first she has to grant the little varmint three unpleasant favors ...
From Jackie Mims Hopkins' *The Horned Toad Prince*

Now it's your turn

Lights! Camera! Action!
Reread your blurb. Use it to identify the most important events in the fairy tale. You are now ready to sketch the "scenes" for the tale's story. Under each sketched scene, jot down brief notes about what you will mention about this event. Use this series of storyboards as a helpful outline as you write the tale. If your retelling of this tale has chapters, each scene may be a separate chapter. Perhaps two or more scenes will fit together well in one chapter.

Make a story map

One way to plan your fairy tale is to think of it the way filmmakers prepare a movie. Before the cameras start shooting, the filmmakers must know the main story episodes. They must also map out the plot (the sequence of events) in a series of sketches called storyboards. You can do this for your fairy tale. The blurb you wrote will help you here.

Novels versus short stories

Once you have worked out the main scenes, or episodes, in your fairy tale, you can decide if you want to tell them briefly in a story or develop each one further as a chapter in a novel. Novels—like short stories—have heroes, villains, and conflicts. Novels have many more characters than short stories, though, and usually have subplots as well as the main plot. Just like a short story, each chapter in a novel has its own beginning, middle, and end. Sometimes chapters in a novel are told from different points of view.

Write a chapter synopsis

Another way to plan a novel is to write a chapter synopsis. If your fairy tale will be novel length, this method might help you tell it. You would group major events into six to 12 categories. You would plan the plot of each category or chapter.

Think about your theme

As you plan your scenes, think about your fairy tale's theme. Is it about being kind to others? Is it about being confident or being honest or loyal? Fairy tales traditionally have contained such messages about the right way to behave. What messages—if any—does your tale send readers?

Tips and techniques
Do not let the length of a novel discourage you from starting one. Sometimes writing a novel takes no more work than writing an excellent short story.

BAIT THE HOOK

You have planned your plot, and you are now ready to enchant readers with your fairy tale. Which kind of magic spell will you use?

Different magical beginnings

You may start your tale before any of its events begin. The words "Once upon a time" are one such traditional fairy tale beginning. This is how "Goldilocks and the Three Bears" begins:

One upon a time, there was a little girl named Goldilocks.

Tips and techniques
Try out different openings for your tale. Just like Goldilocks, you need to experiment to find the one that feels "just right."

Or you might begin your tale in the middle of its events, with a tempting hint of what awaits. This is how Gail Carson Levine begins *Ella Enchanted*, with Ella's first sentences summing up the results of a past event:

That fool of a fairy Lucinda did not intend to lay a curse on me. She meant to bestow a gift. When I cried inconsolably through my first hour of life, my tears were her inspiration.
Gail Carson Levine,
Ella Enchanted

| GETTING STARTED | SETTING THE SCENE | CHARACTERS | VIEWPOINT | SYNOPSES |

Write your opening sentence

Whichever choice you make about where to start your tale, its opening sentences are important. They are the magical charm or hook that will lure readers into your fairy tale world. Here are examples of attention-grabbing opening sentences that work like a charm:

A mysteriously supernatural beginning:

There be this tale told about a tiny fellow who could hide in a foot of shade amid old trees. All that most could see of him was the way he sparkled.
Virginia Hamilton, *The Girl Who Spun Gold*

A surprising and funny beginning:

Once upon a time, in a land where even parents had magic, a mother got so upset with her son's bad temper, sloppy clothes, messy room, and disgusting table manners that she said: "If you're going to act like a beast, you might as well look like one, too."
Vivian Vande Velde, "Beast and Beauty" in *Tales from the Brothers Grimm and the Sisters Weird*

A suspenseful, challenging beginning:

You may think you know this story I am going to tell you, but you have not heard it for true. I was there. So I will tell you the truth of it. Here. Now.
Robert D. San Souci, *Cendrillon: A Caribbean Cinderella*

A beginning with a surprising twist:

Princess Bedelia was as lovely as the moon shining upon a lake full of water-lilies. She was as graceful as a cat leaping. And she was also extremely practical.
Jay Williams, "The Practical Princess" in *The Practical Princess and Other Liberating Fairy Tales*

BUILD THE SUSPENSE

After your wonderful opening, you must not let the magic fade. Keep and build suspense for readers by showing the hero's adventures and hinting at others to come.

A number of adventures

Because people long ago believed that the numbers three and seven had magical significance, these numbers appear in many fairy tales. Heroes often face three dangers or obstacles to overcome. Goldilocks meets three bears, and the Miller's Daughter in "Rumpelstiltskin" must spin gold for three nights. Heroes may also have three or seven magical helpers, too. Snow White has seven dwarfs to help her. Laurence Anholt fractures this fairy tale in his "seriously silly" story about a modern *Snow White and the Seven Aliens*:

> *Snow White dreamed of becoming a pop star. She wanted to be number one in the charts, just like her hero, Hank Hunk from Boysbop.*
> Laurence Anholt, *Snow White and the Seven Aliens*

Use this fairy tale tradition to plot out three or seven exciting adventures for your hero. In Donna Jo Napoli's *The Prince of the Pond*, the Frog Prince faces many natural dangers before he again meets his worst enemy—the witch who turned him into a frog.

Hint at danger

You can also add suspense by hinting about what is to come. This writing technique—called foreshadowing—will have readers eagerly turning pages to find out what happens next. In Robin McKinley's *Beauty*, Beauty discovers a dying rose after she delays her return to Beast. Its brown petals hint at Beast's condition. Readers then rush along with Beauty to find out his fate. In novel-length tales, authors sometimes keep suspense high by ending chapters with foreshadowing. Gail Carson Levine uses this technique when she had Ella remark at the end of one chapter, "But I had no luck." Readers just have to turn the page to find out what happens next!

Tips and techniques

Start small and build up to the most challenging adventures for your hero. This will keep readers from feeling let down.

A race against time

One way to keep readers on the edge of their seats is to place characters in a race against time. Cinderella only has until midnight before her coach turns back into a pumpkin and her dress into rags. In Robin McKinley's *Beauty*, Beauty has only seven days to spend with her family before gentle Beast begins to die.

END WITH A BANG

Stories build up suspense until they reach a climax. After this dramatic point, the characters' main problems are solved. In a traditional fairy tale, the hero has learned something, conquered an enemy, or earned a reward. Often, everyone lives "happily ever after." If you have written a fractured fairy tale, though, the ending may surprise readers. A hero may go back to her old life, having learned something unpleasant about herself or without the reward she expected. Another hero may have his own, unexpected definition of happiness.

The climax

A fairy tale's climax is often very dramatic. It tops off the suspense with a scene where action produces strong emotions in the characters. In *Ella Enchanted*, the climax comes when her stepsister Hattie rips Ella's mask from her face at the ball. Revealing Ella's true identity that way causes shock, fright, anger, and delight. In *The Magic Circle*, the climax occurs when the shocked children learn that the old woman is a witch. Fire does not burn her, and her bitten-off tongue does not bleed. In *Hansel and Gretel*, Gretel tricks the witch and pushes her into the oven, thus saving her brother and herself.

Conclude your adventure

Have your hero finish her adventure or journey. Like Robin McKinley's Beauty or Gail Carson Levine's Ella, this conclusion may be a totally happy one for your character. As Ella says at the end of the book:

> *Decisions were a delight after the curse. I loved having the power to say yes or no, and refusing anything was a special pleasure. My contrariness kept Char laughing, and his goodness kept me in love. And so, with laughter and love, we lived happily ever after.*
> Gail Carson Levine, *Ella Enchanted*

Such a happy ending will delight and charm readers of your traditional fairy tale. But if you are writing a fractured fairy tale, you will want a different kind of spellbinding ending.

Tips and techniques
Put together a fractured fairy tale by combining the events and characters of two different tales.

Create mixed emotions

Donna Jo Napoli's ending in *The Prince of the Pond* is bittersweet. The prince becomes human again, but he and his frog family lose one another:

> *The human man reached out his hands toward the froglets. I thought he was going to catch them. But he didn't touch them. He merely reached out his hands and sighed. "Good-bye, my little froglets. Goodbye, my sweet children." He looked toward the grass with searching eyes. "Good-bye, frog wife. Best possible wife. I love you. Try to remember me. Good-bye, good-bye."*
> Donna Jo Napoli, *The Prince of the Pond*

Your fairy tale might also have an ending that is both happy and sad.

AVOID BEING PREDICTABLE

Surprise your readers. Diane Stanley's Rumpelstiltskin's daughter turns down the chance to marry the king and instead becomes his prime minister. When the Horned Toad Prince becomes human again, he refuses to marry bad-tempered and dishonest Reba. You might even choose to tickle readers' funny bones by combining two fairy tales into one. This is what Jon Scieszka does at the end of "Cinderrumpelstiltskin or the Girl Who Really Blew It." Arthur Levine uses this technique in *The Boardwalk Princess*, too.

Endings that suggest new beginnings

A good ending often refers back in some way to the beginning of the story. This reminds readers of how much has or has not changed since the tale started. Princess Bedelia in *The Practical Princess* is about to start a new life with the hairy prince she has rescued, but she has not changed her nature:

> *And of course, since Bedelia had rescued him from captivity, she married him. First, however, she made him get a haircut and a shave so that she could see what he really looked like. For she was always practical.*
> Jay Williams, "The Practical Princess" in *The Practical Princess and Other Liberating Fairy Tales*

Bedelia and her prince will be able to depend on her practicality throughout their new life together.

Now it's your turn

Choose your own ending

Reread one of your favorite fairy tales and think about its ending. Could it have ended in other ways? Write one of these new endings. Put it aside for a while. Then go back and read both versions of the tale. Which one do you prefer— and why? Could your own fairy tale have more than one ending? Take 10 minutes to brainstorm two possible endings for your tale.

Bad endings

To create a fairy tale that leaves readers feeling enchanted, avoid a bad ending.

Bad endings are ones that:

- fizzle out or end abruptly because you've run out of ideas
- fail to show how the characters have changed in some way

MAKE YOUR WORDS WORK

Your well-chosen words will work magic. They will transport readers to fairy-tale worlds where astonishing events and creatures seem as real as next-door neighbors. Every word counts. Just as you would not waste magic wishes, choose your words wisely. Only the most vivid and powerful words are worthy of your tale.

A sense of life

Make your descriptions come alive. Touch and hearing as well as sight help readers experience Beauty's first impressions of Beast's enchanted forest:

It was cool here without being cold; sunlight dripped a little way among the leaves, but without warmth. Most of the tree trunks were straight and smooth to a height above our heads, where the broad branches began. I heard water running somewhere; except for that, and the noises of our passage—harness jingling and squeaking and occasional patches of cobweb ice that shattered underfoot—the woods were perfectly still.
Robin McKinley, *Beast*

Use vivid imagery

Use your imagination to create vivid word pictures with metaphors and similes. In *Ella Enchanted*, Ella uses a metaphor to describe how she feels while bravely trying to disobey a command:

> *The tears streaming from my eyes were acid, burning my cheeks.*
> Gail Carson Levine, *Ella Enchanted*

This does not mean that Ella's tears really were a strong chemical that destroyed her flesh. It is a word picture that communicates how intense her emotional pain was then.

In *Cinderellis and the Glass Hill*, the author uses a simile to describe the results of Ellis' magical powders:

> *Using more balancing powder and a pinch of extra-strength powder, he stacked the tomatoes in the shape of a giant tomato and the beets in the shape of a giant beet. His masterpiece was the carrots, rising like a ballerina from a tiny tiny tip.*
> Gail Carson Levine, *Cinderellis and the Glass Hill*

This word picture comparing the giant, upright carrot to a ballerina on tiptoe helps readers imagine its shape and size more vividly.

Tips and techniques
A metaphor describes something by calling it something else—for instance, a fierce man is a "tiger." A simile describes something by comparing it to something else with the word "like" or "as." For example, a dewdrop sparkles like a diamond.

WRITE TO EXCITE

When you write action scenes, excite your readers with your word choice. Replace everyday action words with bold, unusual ones. Have characters race instead of run and leap instead of jump.

Jay Williams uses vivid action words along with a simile when describing how Petronella rescues a surprisingly lazy and unwilling prince:

> *She grabbed him by the wrist and dragged him out of bed. She hauled him down the stairs. His horse and hers were in a separate stable, and she saddled them quickly. She gave the prince a shove, and he mounted. She jumped on her own horse, seized the prince's reins, and away they went like the wind.*
>
> Jay Williams, "Petronella" in *The Practical Princess and Other Liberating Fairy Tales*

Instead of *took*, Williams uses the more exciting words *grabbed, dragged, hauled,* and *seized.*

Now it's your turn

Imagine that!
Here's something you can do alone or with a friend. Brainstorm some similes for colors and textures. Make a list of 10 colors and textures. For each word, write down five similes. For instance, "As red (or blue or green) as a …" or try "As smooth (or sharp or rough) as the …" How could you use these images or ones like them in your fairy tale? Use a dictionary or thesaurus for extra help.

Now it's your turn

Seize the day!

By yourself or with a friend, make a list of 10 everyday actions words such as walk or fly. Then have fun brainstorming at least four unusual substitutes for each word. Perhaps an evil stepmother would glare instead of look. Maybe a dragon would bellow instead of roar. Use a dictionary or thesaurus for extra help.

Use dramatic irony

When your readers know something the characters do not, suspense increases. This is called dramatic irony, and authors strengthen it by choosing words wisely. After Hansel and Gretel discover the witch's cottage, readers shudder. Gretel's innocent remarks increase our tension:

> *And the cottage is so beautiful. I cannot believe how beautiful it is. It is like heaven itself.*
> Donna Jo Napoli, *The Magic Circle*

Using dramatic irony is another way to cast a spell over your readers.

Remember—make every word count. Words will help you win your own fairy tale reward: eager and happy readers of your tales.

USE DRAMATIC DIALOGUE

Conversations can help readers understand different personalities and the relationships between people. Dialogue also gives readers' eyes a rest as it breaks up the page of narrative (storytelling). Done well, dialogue is a powerful storytelling tool—one that adds color, mood, and suspense even as it moves the plot forward.

Let your characters speak for themselves

Early in *Ella Enchanted*, a conversation between Ella and her future stepsisters reveals what the other two teens are like and how one sister bullies the other:

> *"Would you like something to eat?"*
> *"Ye—" Olive began, but her sister interrupted firmly.*
> *"Oh, no. No thank you. We never eat at parties. The excitement quite takes away our appetites."*
> *"My appetite—" Olive tried again.*
> *"Our appetites are small. Mother worries. But it looks delicious."*
> *Hattie edged toward the food. "Quail eggs are such a delicacy. Ten brass KJs apiece. Olive, there are fifty at least."*
> Gail Carson Levine, *Ella Enchanted*

Hattie's self-centeredness and the sisters' interest in the cost of things are important plot elements in this fairy tale novel.

Now it's your turn

Listen in

Tune in to the way people talk. Turn on the radio or TV for 10 minutes, and copy down bits of conversation. Or jot down what you overhear in the hallway at school or in an elevator or store. You will begin to notice how people often have favorite expressions and different rhythms to their speech. Sometimes, someone may not wait to talk until the other person is finished! How can you use these different speech patterns in the dialogue you write?

Follow convention

Dialogue is usually written down according to certain rules. Each new speaker begins a new paragraph. You already know that what a person actually said is enclosed in quotation marks, followed or preceded by a tag such as "he said" or "she said." Sometimes, to give the sense of a real conversation, writers place these tags in the middle of a sentence. This placement adds another rhythm to the conversation, making it more lifelike.

Tips and techniques

Use say, said, or wrote to introduce quotations. You can sometimes substitute words such as complained, whispered, or shouted for variety and when they suit the situation.

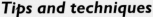

ADDING COLOR AND MOOD

Donna Jo Napoli uses dialogue to add color and mood to the adventures of the Frog Prince. He is so shocked by his transformation that he is silent while the female frog lectures him:

> *"Can't you tell a toad from a frog?"*
> *He shook his head.*
> *Now I leaned toward him. "Oh me, oh me, oh me, oh me. How on earth have you survived so long without knowing that?" I stared at him. He didn't answer.*
> *"Well, you certainly won't last very long around this pond if you don't learn fast," I said.*
> *I cleared my throat and spoke in my most commanding voice. "A toad has dry, warty skin." I looked hard at him. "A frog has wet, smooth skin. Got that?"*
> *He blinked.*
> *"A toad has bean-shaped bumps behind his eyes and sometimes even between his eyes and other places, too. A frog has, at most, lovely folds of skin here or there."*
> *He blinked.*
>
> Donna Jo Napoli, *The Prince of the Pond*

The Frog Prince's silence is a humorous contrast to the enjoyment the female frog seems to take in giving him all the details of a frog's appearance. He is probably much less delighted than she is to have "lovely folds of skin"!

Now it's your turn

Compress your dialogue

Try removing tags such as "he said" or "she shouted" from your dialogue. Does the pace of the conversation seem more natural? Does this pace better suit the mood and purpose of the scene? Can you still identify who is speaking? Some scenes work better with compressed dialogue that has no tags. If you cannot tell who is speaking without tags, you may want to work more to develop each character's voice.

| GETTING STARTED | SETTING THE SCENE | CHARACTERS | VIEWPOINT | SYNOPSES |

Now it's your turn

As she was saying …

Reread your fairy tale. Are there parts of the narrative that could be better told in dialogue? Rewrite a scene using or adding dialogue. If they are appropriate, use overlapping statements or humor. Now set both versions of the tale aside. Go back later to see which version you like more.

CASE STUDY

For many years, Virginia Hamilton collected and retold African and African-American tales. *The Girl Who Spun Gold* is her version of the West Indian Rumpelstiltskin story. In this tale, Hamilton captures the casual, musical style of West Indian speech patterns.

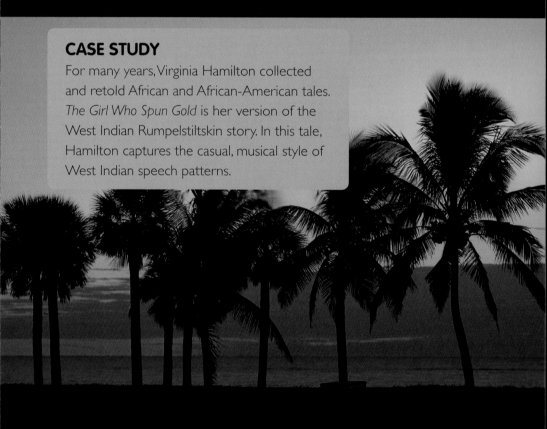

USE DIFFERENT VOICES

Writing dialogue is a challenge even for experienced, skilled writers. Remember that characters should not sound like you. How characters speak often reveals a great deal about their background.

Here are examples of how people's speech differs in vocabulary, rhythm, accent, and pronunciation:

A dialect of English:
Quashie uses vocabulary, rhythms, and the accent typical of English spoken in the West Indies:

> *"Never you mind, Mama," Queenie Quashi said. "Never you sorrow, my dearie-dear. You will see. Big King-mahn will forget about it, the golden stuff he wants me to spin be such a long time coming."*
> Virginia Hamilton, *The Girl Who Spun Gold*

Tips and techniques
Use speech patterns to clearly identify minor characters. Someone might stutter. Another character might have an accent. Whenever that character speaks, show this foreign accent by spelling an everyday word differently.

CASE STUDY
Donna Jo Napoli used her training as a professor of linguistics to create De Fawg Pin's (The Frog Prince's) speech problems. She made him miss all the sounds that people make using the mouth part called the hard palate.

A speech defect:
This Frog Prince cannot pronounce the sounds of the letters l, r, and s:

> *Pin looked at me. "I tode you. I'm not me. I can't expain any betteh."* He hung his head.
> Donna Jo Napoli, *The Prince of the Pond*

A combination of cultures:
Throughout the American Southwest, Spanish as well as English is spoken. Often daily speech contains words from both languages:

> *"Many, many years ago when I came to this country, I offended the great spirit of the arroyo. The spirit put a spell on me and turned me into a horned toad. For many years I've been waiting for a cowgirl like you to break the spell. Muchas gracias for my freedom, senorita. Now I'll be leaving as I promised."*
> Jackie Mims Hopkins,
> *The Horned Toad Prince*

Supernatural origin:
Ella translates one of the nonhuman languages Gail Carson Levine invents for fairy tale creatures:

> *"forns uiv eMMong FFnOO ehf nushOOn," he growled. ("It will taste sour for hours.") I was an it—I had studied sufficient Ogrese to understand almost everything.*
> Gail Carson Levine, *Ella Enchanted*

Tips and techniques
Create a fairy tale language for one of your creatures. Suggest that English is not this creature's native language by including a foreign word or two in a greeting or excited remark.

Tips and techniques
Watch out! Your slang may not fit well into a fairy tale set long ago or far away. If you are deliberately fracturing a tale, though, slang may be a useful tool.

BEAT WRITER'S BLOCK

Even talented, professional writers sometimes fall under the "evil spell" called writer's block. That is when a writer is stuck for words or ideas at the beginning or in the middle of a story. Never fear! There are ways to undo this spell—and they work like a charm!

Ignore your inner critic

Do not listen to that inner voice that might be whispering negative ideas about your writing. All writers experience some failures and rejection. Thirty-two publishers rejected Vivian Vande Velde's first book. Gail Carson Levine sent manuscripts to editors for nine years before one was finally accepted. Levine says, "Kids abandon stories all the time." She tells young writers, "It is more worthwhile to stick with a story and revise it and try to finish it than abandon ship. Revisions, for any writer, are the name of the game."

Laurence Anholt, author of fractured fairy tales such as *Snow White and the Seven Aliens*, would agree. He says, "Rewriting is simply the most important process. I think of writing as similar to working with clay—you add pieces and remove huge chunks. It's a flexible process and you have to be quite ruthless about removing excess chunks."

No ideas

If you have been following the writer's golden rule (writing regularly and often), you already have a powerful weapon against writer's block. Professional authors fight and win this battle, too.

Vivian Vande Velde says, "If I work a little bit every day, I get a lot more ideas than I do if I sit around just waiting for those ideas." She tells new writers, "Thinking about your story doesn't count. Try to write at least one page. If—the next day—you decide you hate it, you can always tear it up and start over."

Philip Pullman keeps to his goal of three written pages a day. "If you are stuck," he says, "you just write three bad pages. It doesn't matter. ... There are three pages there that weren't there yesterday." When he is faced with a hard decision between two writing choices—such as the order of events in a story—Pullman goes out for coffee at a café. Sitting and thinking about his writing problem in this different environment helps him.

Now it's your turn

A character-building activity

Stuck in the middle of your story? Follow the authors' advice—just write! You'll get to know your characters better. Ask yourself what makes a character angry, happy, or embarrassed. Now have this character write you a letter complaining about the story or other characters.

CASE STUDY

Be open to inspiration. Robin McKinley never imagined that she would write two novels retelling the tale of "Beauty and the Beast." McKinley moved to England, though, where she has a huge garden with 300 rosebushes. After five years of gardening there, she began to think about how her increased knowledge of roses might fit into a new tale. She wrote *Rose Daughter* in six months of intense effort.

A WRITERS' GROUP

Writing may seem lonely. Some writers find that the "magic potion" to cure this loneliness is belonging to a writers' group. They meet regularly in person or over the Internet with "writing buddies." These critique groups help fight writer's block by sharing ideas, experiences, and even goals. Vivian Vande Velde belongs to two different writers' groups in her community. Laurence Arnholt "bounces ideas" off his wife, Catherine, an artist who illustrates some of his books.

Tips and techniques
To get fresh ideas, take a break in a different environment to think through a writing problem. Or just take a break.

Role play

Another way to beat loneliness as a writer is to involve your family or friends. Turn your writing problem into a game with them. Give each person a character role from your story, and see what ideas and dialogue turn up!

Build character

Friends and family can help through another game. Sit in a circle. Write a character's name on a large sheet of paper, and describe this character to the other players. Pass the sheet around quickly, giving everyone just a minute or two to write down something about the character. This might be what the character looks like, thinks, used to do, or even dreams. Keep going around the circle until you have 15 items written down. Then have fun reading these ideas aloud.

Now it's your turn

Break the evil spell of writer's block with other writers!
Start a writer's group with other writers, or partner up with a writing buddy. Set a regular meeting time and place, and talk about how much new work you will bring to meetings.

TAKE THE NEXT STEP

Congratulations! Completing your own fairy tale is a fantastic achievement. You have learned a lot about writing and probably about yourself, too. You are now ready to take the next step in creating wonderful new stories.

Another fairy tale?

While writing this fairy tale, you might have had ideas for another one. Perhaps you completed a traditional tale and now want to try a fractured one. Perhaps you wrote your first tale from the hero's point of view but now want to try one told by the villain or a minor character. Perhaps writing a fairy tale set in a different culture or part of the world interests you.

How about a sequel?

Is there more to tell about the characters in your completed fairy tale? Maybe further adventures await them. Donna Jo Napoli followed up *The Prince of the Pond* with two sequels. The first book—titled *Jimmy, the Pickpocket of the Palace*—tells what happens to the Frog Prince's froglet son Jimmy when he arrives at the Prince's palace. The second sequel—titled *Gracie: The Pixie of the Puddle*—tells the story of Jimmy's frog friend Gracie.

Gail Carson Levine's latest book, titled *Fairest*, follows the family of Ella's friend Areida, who lives in the land of Ayortha. It is a retelling of the fairy tale "Snow White and the Seven Dwarfs," although it does not have the familiar ending.

CASE STUDY

Gail Carson Levine has written a series of short novels fracturing traditional fairy tales. Besides *Cinderellis and the Glass Hill*, this series includes *The Fairy's Mistake*, *The Princess Test*, *Princess Sonora and the Long Sleep*, *For Biddle's Sake*, and *The Fairy's Return*. All of these novels are set in the imaginary kingdom of Biddle.

Tips and techniques
Use the fairy tale setting of a tale you have written or read as the setting of your next story.

Now it's your turn

Imagine that!

Brainstorm your next story with pen and paper. Think of a fairy tale you enjoyed reading. Or grab one you have never read from the library. List five things that might have happened to the hero or creatures after or even before the events described in the tale. Do not worry about punctuation or grammar as you jot down ideas. Repeat this process with another tale. When you are done, you may have found the characters and plot for your next writing project.

LEARN FROM THE AUTHORS

You can learn a great deal from the advice of successful writers. Almost all will tell you that success without hard work and occasional failure is just a fairy tale! Even though few writers earn enough from their books to make a living, they value their ability to create and communicate through written words.

Donna Jo Napoli

Donna Jo Napoli (left) grew up in a poor family that did not own books. She was also slow to learn to read, since she had vision problems that no one recognized until she was 10 years old. After that, using resources from school and the library, Napoli quickly began to make up for lost time. She says of her childhood, "Books opened up my world."

Napoli says that writing and other arts help people "explore parts of our feelings and hopes and dreams that we don't allow for in our daily work and responsibilities to others. We can be better—and what a joy that is." She knows that one day her many writing projects will include a Chinese and an African fairy tale.

Gail Carson Levine

This award-winning author struggled with her most recent work, a novel titled *Fairest*. She spent four years writing this version of "Snow White and the Seven Dwarfs," with about eight months off during this period to finish other projects. While writing *Fairest*, Levine switched points of view four times. She completed about 300 pages each time before she found the viewpoint that worked for her.

When she reads fairy tales she wants to retell, Levine says that she looks "for leaps of logic and gaps in the story." She tells kids that as an experienced writer, she expects writing "to be difficult. I expect to have to inch along sometimes."

Jon Scieszka

Jon Scieszka says, "My ideas come from all different things: my kids, kids I've taught, kids I've learned from, watching movies, playing with my cat, talking to my wife, staring out the window, and about a million other places. But what turns the ideas into stories and books is sitting down and writing and rewriting and throwing away writing and writing some more. That's the hard part. I never know exactly how long it takes to write a story. I read a lot of stuff, think about different stories all the time, scribble things down on paper, type them up, change them, scribble again, think some more, add things … ."

Robert D. San Souci

Robert D. San Souci (right) loved to read fairy tales and folk tales when he was a kid. He grew up in a home filled with books. San Souci was shy, and writing was a way to express himself.

In second grade, San Souci wrote his first book, which his brother Daniel illustrated. Today Daniel San Souci is a professional artist who often illustrates his brother's books.

San Souci gets ideas for books from reading, researching in the library, traveling, and just watching and listening to people. He says that even a simple bus ride sometimes inspires him as he sits and looks out the window. He says, "I feel privileged to be a writer."

Robin McKinley

Robin McKinley says that writing "is the hardest work I know—my usual metaphor is that it's harder than digging out old tree stumps with a pickax, and I speak from experience. The story is always better than your ability to write it. My belief about this is that if you ever get to the point that you think you've done a story justice, you're in the wrong business. Time to trade in your word processor and become a baker or a mechanic." She advises new writers, "Read as much as you can and write as much as you can. Reading feeds your own storytelling, and writing, like anything worth doing well, needs practice. It needs practice *practice* **practice** PRACTICE."

Let your fairy tale rest in your desk drawer or on a shelf for several weeks. Then, when you read it through, you will have fresh eyes to spot any flaws.

Edit your work

Reading your work aloud is one way to make the writing crisper. Now is the time to check spelling and punctuation. When the fairy tale is as good as it can be, write it out again or type it up on the computer. This is your manuscript.

Think of a title

Great titles capture the reader's interest. They not only indicate the subject of the book but also make the reader want to learn more about it. *Snow White and the Seven Aliens* is a more compelling title than *A New Version of Snow White*. Sometimes titles also indicate the author's voice. Jon Scieszka's title *The Stinky Cheese Man and Other Fairly Stupid Tales* reflects the joking and casual way this writer retells traditional fairy tales.

Be professional

If you have a computer, you can type up your manuscript to give it a professional presentation. Manuscripts should always be printed on one side of white paper, with wide margins and double spacing. Pages should be numbered, and new chapters should start

on a new page. You should also include your title as a header on the top of each page. At the front, you should have a title page with your name, address, telephone number, and e-mail address on it. Repeat this information on the last page.

Make your own book

If your school has its own computer lab, why not use it to publish your fairy tale? A computer will let you choose your own font (print style) or justify the text (making margins even like a professionally printed page). When you have typed and saved the fairy tale to a file, you can edit it quickly with the spelling and grammar checker, or move sections around using the cut-and-paste tool, which saves a lot of rewriting. A graphics program will let you design and print a cover for the book, too.

Having the fairy tale on a computer file also means you can print a copy whenever you need one or revise the whole tale if you want to.

Tips and techniques
Always make a copy of your fairy tale before you give it to others to read. Otherwise, if they lose it, you may have lost all your valuable work.

The next step is to find an audience for your tale. Family members or classmates may be receptive. Members of a community group such as a **Girl Scout troop** or a senior citizens center might like to read your work. Or you may want to share your work through a Web site, a literary magazine, or publishing house.

Some places to publish your fairy tale

There are several magazines and writing Web sites that accept fairy tales from young authors. Some give writing advice and run regular competitions. Each site has its own rules about submitting work, so remember to read these carefully. Here are two more ideas:

- Send the fairy tale to your school newspaper.
- Watch your local newspaper or magazines for writing competitions you could enter.

Finding a publisher

Study the market to find out which publishers publish fairy tales. Addresses of publishers and information about whether they accept submissions can be found in writers' handbooks in your local library. Remember that manuscripts that haven't been asked for or paid for by a publisher—called unsolicited manuscripts—are rarely published.

Getting it ready

Secure any submission with a staple or paper clip and always enclose a short letter (explaining what you have sent) and a stamped, self-addressed envelope for the tale's return.

Writer's tip

Don't lose heart if an editor rejects your fairy tale. See this as a chance to make your work better and try again. Remember, having your work published is wonderful, but it is not the only thing. Being able to write a fairy tale is an accomplishment that will delight the people you love. Talk about it with your younger brother or sister. Read it to your grandfather. Find your audience.

Some final words

You are now a member of a great storytelling tradition. People around the world for generations have told fairy tales. You have shown that you too can write a tale that communicates pleasure in fantasy and presents ideas about what is good and bad behavior. With this success and knowledge, you are ready to set out on the next spellbinding adventure in your life!

Read! Write!

And keep your sense of enchantment alive.

Glossary

back story—the history of characters and events that happened before the story begins

chapter synopsis—an outline that describes briefly what happens in each chapter

dramatic irony—when the reader knows something the characters don't

edit—to remove all unnecessary words from your story, correcting errors, and rewriting the text until the story is the best it can be

editor—the person at a publishing house who finds new books to publish and advises authors on how to improve their stories by telling them what needs to be added or cut

first-person viewpoint—a viewpoint that allows a single character to tell the story as if he or she had written it; readers feel as if that character is talking directly to them

foreshadowing—dropping hints of coming events or dangers that are essential to the outcome of the story

genres—categories of writing characterized by a particular style, form, or content

manuscript—book or article typed or written by hand

metaphor—a figure of speech that paints a word picture; calling a man "a mouse" is a metaphor from which we learn in one word that the man is timid or weak, not that he is actually a mouse

motives—the reasons why a character does something

narrative—the telling of a story

omniscient viewpoint—an all-seeing narrator who can describe all the characters and tell readers how they are acting and feeling

plot—sequence of events that drives a story forward; the problems that the hero must resolve

point of view—the eyes through which a story is told

publisher—a person or company who pays for an author's manuscript to be printed as a book and who distributes and sells that book

sequel—a story that carries an existing one forward

simile—saying something is like something else, a word picture, such as "clouds like frayed lace"

synopsis—short summary that describes what a story is about and introduces the main characters

theme—the main issue that the story addresses, such as good versus evil, the importance of truth, and so on; a story can have more than one theme

third-person viewpoint—a viewpoint that describes the events of the story through a single character's eyes

unsolicited manuscripts—manuscripts that are sent to publishers without being requested; these submissions usually end up in the "slush pile," where they may wait a long time to be read

writer's block—when writers think they can no longer write or have used up all their ideas

Further information

Visit your local libraries and make friends with the librarians. They can direct you to useful sources of information, including magazines that publish young people's short fiction. You can learn your craft and read great stories at the same time.

Librarians will also know if any published authors are scheduled to speak in your area. Many authors visit schools and offer writing workshops. Ask your teacher to invite a favorite author to speak at your school.

On the Web

For more information on this topic, use FactHound.
1. Go to www.facthound.com
2. Type in this book ID: 0756533694
3. Click on the *Fetch It* button.
FactHound will find the best Web sites for you.

Read all the Write Your Own books

Write Your Own Adventure Story
Write Your Own Biography
Write Your Own Fairy Tale
Write Your Own Fantasy Story
Write Your Own Historical Fiction Story
Write Your Own Mystery Story
Write Your Own Myth
Write Your Own Realistic Fiction Story
Write Your Own Science Fiction Story
Write Your Own Tall Tale

Read more fairy tales

Andersen, Hans Christian. *The Little Mermaid.* New York: Minedition/Penguin, 2005.
Anholt, Laurence. *Eco-Wolf and the Three Pigs.* Minneapolis: Compass Point Books, 2004.
Climo, Shirley. *The Korean Cinderella.* New York: HarperCollins Publishers, 1993.
Garcia, Laura Gallego. *The Legend of the Wandering King.* New York: Arthur A. Levine Books, 2005.
Hopkins, Jackie Mims. *The Gold Miner's Daughter: A Melodramatic Fairy Tale.* Atlanta: Peachtree Publishers, 2006.
Levine, Arthur A. *The Boardwalk Princess.* New York: Tambourine Books, 1993.
Levine, Gail Carson. *Fairest.* New York: HarperCollins, 2006.
Levine, Gail Carson. *Princess Sonora and the Long Sleep.* New York: HarperCollins, 1999.
Louie, Ai-ling. *Yeh-Shen: A Cinderella Story from China.* New York: Philomel Books, 1982.
McCaughrean, Geraldine. *One Thousand and One Arabian Nights.* Oxford: Oxford University Press, 1999.
McKinley, Robin. *Rose Daughter.* New York: Greenwillow Books, 1997.
Napoli, Donna Jo. *Gracie: The Pixie of the Puddle.* New York: Dutton Children's Books, 2004.
Napoli, Donna Jo. *Jimmy, the Pickpocket of the Palace.* New York: Dutton Children's Books, 1995.
Opie, Iona, and Peter Opie. *The Classic Fairy Tales.* Oxford: Oxford University Press, 1992.
Philip, Neil. *The Illustrated Book of Fairy Tales: Spellbinding Stories From Around the World.* New York: DK Publishing, 1997.
Pullman, Philip. *I Was a Rat!* New York: Knopf, 2000.
San Souci, Robert. D. *Sootface: An Ojibwa Cinderella Story.* New York: Delacorte Press, 1994.
Sanderson, Ruth. *Rose Red & Snow White: A Grimms Fairy Tale.* Boston: Little, Brown, 1997.
Scieszka, Jon. *The True Story of the Three Little Pigs by A. Wolf.* New York: Viking Kestrel, 1989.
Scieszka, Jon, and Lane Smith. *The Stinky Cheese Man and Other Fairly Stupid Tales.* New York: Viking, 1992.
Young, Ed. *Lon Po Po: A Red-Riding Hood Story From China.* New York: Philomel Books, 1989.

Books cited

Andersen, Hans Christian. *Fairy Tales of Hans Christian Andersen*. New York: Viking, 1995.

Anholt, Laurence. *Snow White and the Seven Aliens*. Minneapolis: Compass Point Books, 2004.

Brothers Grimm. *Grimm's Fairy Tales: Twenty Stories*. New York: Viking, 1973.

Garner, Alan. *Alan Garner's Books of British Fairy Tales*. New York: Delacorte Press, 1984.

Hamilton, Virginia. *The Girl Who Spun Gold*. New York: Blue Sky Press, 2000.

Hopkins, Jackie Mims. *The Horned Toad Prince*. Atlanta: Peachtree, 2000.

Levine, Gail Carson. *Cinderellis and the Glass Hill*. New York: HarperCollins, 2000.

Levine, Gail Carson. *Ella Enchanted*. New York: HarperCollins, 1997.

McKinley, Robin. *Beauty: A Retelling of the Story of Beauty & The Beast*. New York: Harper & Row, 1978.

Napoli, Donna Jo. *Beast*. New York: Atheneum Books for Young Readers, 2000.

Napoli, Donna Jo. *The Magic Circle*. New York: Dutton Children's Books, 1993.

Napoli, Donna Jo. *The Prince of the Pond: Otherwise Known as De Fawg Pin*. New York: Dutton Children's Books, 1992.

Perrault, Charles. *The Complete Fairy Tales of Charles Perrault*. Trans. Neil Philip. New York: Clarion Books, 1993.

Pollock, Penny. *The Turkey Girl: A Zuni Cinderella Story*. Boston: Little, Brown, 1996.

San Souci, Robert. D. *Cendrillon: A Caribbean Cinderella*. Simon & Schuster, 1998.

Stanley, Diane. *Rumpelstiltskin's Daughter*. New York: Morrow Junior Books, 1997.

Vande Velde, Vivian. *Tales from the Brothers Grimm and the Sisters Weird*. Orlando, Fla.: Magic Carpet Books, 2005.

Williams, Jay. *The Practical Princess, and Other Liberating Fairy Tales*. New York: Parents' Magazine Press, 1978.

Image credits

Svetlana Zhurkin, cover, 12 (bottom), 20, 24 (bottom), 33 (bottom), 49 (bottom); Rafa Irusta/Shutterstock, back cover (top); Brand X Pictures, back cover (bottom), 18; Mikhail Blajenov/Dreamstime, 1; John Cross/The Free Press, 2; Profimedia International s.r.o./Alamy, 4; Faringdon Collection, Buscot, Oxon, UK/The Bridgeman Art Library, 5; David Davis/Shutterstock, 6 (top); Polina Lobanova/Shutterstock, 6 (bottom); Lori Martin/Shutterstock, 7 (top); Don Maclellan/Corbis Sygma, 7 (bottom); Brooke Fasani/Photonica/Getty Images, 8; Blue Lantern Studio/Corbis, 9 (top), 10 (bottom), 21, 32, 34 (bottom), 37 (top), 53 (top); Vasiliy Koval/Shutterstock, 9 (bottom), 64; Jason Stitt/Shutterstock, 10 (top); Viktor Pryymachuk/Shutterstock, 11; Mary Evans Picture Library, 12 (top), 23 (top), 34 (top), 61; Cathy Keifer/Shutterstock, 13; Ryan Klos/Shutterstock, 14 (top); Roman Ivaschenko/Shutterstock, 14 (bottom); Kristian Sekulic/Shutterstock, 15; Marc C. Johnson/Shutterstock, 16 (top); Rob Brimson/Taxi/Getty Images, 16 (bottom); Bluestocking/Shutterstock, 17 (top); Jim Lopes/Shutterstock, 17 (bottom); Tatiana Popova/Shutterstock, 19; Historical Picture Archive/Corbis, 22; Alvaro Pantoja/Shutterstock, 23 (bottom); Ronen/Shutterstock, 24 (top); Bildarchiv Preussischer Kulturbesitz/Art Resource, N.Y., 25 (top); The Granger Collection, New York, 25 (bottom); Miramax/Everett/Rex USA, 26, 35 (top); Atli Mar/Nordic Photos/Getty Images, 27 (top); Robert Hardholt/Shutterstock, 27 (bottom); Tamara Kulikova/Shutterstock, 28 (top); Feng Yu/Shutterstock, 28 (bottom); Images/Corbis, 30 (top); Leonard de Selva/Corbis, 30 (bottom), 42; Stephen Coburn/Shutterstock, 31 (top), 57 (bottom); Tatiana Grozetskaya/Shutterstock, 31 (bottom); Scott Rothstein/Shutterstock, 33 (top); Colin & Linda McKie/Shutterstock, 35 (bottom); Ana Blazic/Shutterstock, 36 (top); Valentin Mosichev/Shutterstock, 36 (bottom); Edyta Pawlowska/Shutterstock, 37 (bottom), 59; Egor Mopanko/Shutterstock, 38 (top); V. J. Matthew/Shutterstock, 38 (bottom); Signorina/Shutterstock, 39 (left); Oleg Vladimirovich Filipchuk/Shutterstock, 39 (right); Galina Barskaya/Shutterstock, 40 (top); Vera Bogaerts/Shutterstock, 40 (bottom); Linda Bucklin/Shutterstock, 41 (top); Lorelyn Medina/Shutterstock, 41 (bottom); Chris Clinton/Taxi/Getty Images, 43 (top); Mandy Godbehear/Shutterstock, 43 (bottom); Michelle D. Milliman/Shutterstock, 44 (top), 49 (top); Paul-André Belle-Isle/Shutterstock, 44 (bottom); Dana Heinemann/Shutterstock, 45 (top); Frank Boellmann/Shutterstock, 45 (bottom); Gen Nishino/Taxi/Getty Images, 46; ANP/Shutterstock, 47 (top); Paulaphoto/Shutterstock, 47 (bottom), 60; Tina Rencelj/Shutterstock, 48 (top); Frederic Tousche/Photographer's Choice/Getty Images, 48 (bottom); eStock Photo/Alamy, 50 (top); Jaimie Duplass/Shutterstock, 50 (bottom); ImageState/Alamy, 51 (top); Andrey Valerevich Kiselev/Shutterstock, 51 (bottom); Hummer/Taxi/Getty Images, 52; Charles Maraia/Taxi/Getty Images, 53 (bottom); Barry Furrow, 54; Robert D. San Souci's Home Page, 55; David Young-Wolff/Alamy, 56 (top); Alexey Utemov/Shutterstock, 56 (bottom); Phil Boorman/Taxi/Getty Images, 57 (top); Stock4B/Getty Images, 58 (top); Ebby May/Taxi/Getty Images, 58 (bottom); Sharon Meredith/Shutterstock, 62.

Index